BE A PERSON OF IMPACT!

12 Strategies to be the CEO of Your Future

For multiple copies and bulk orders, please contact our office
T: 619.624.9691 E: info@freibergs.com

Published by freibergs.com, a San Diego Consulting Group, Inc. company and Create Space.com Copyright © 2015 San Diego Consulting Group, Inc.

ISBN-13: 978-1511852289
ISBN-10: 1511852283

Design and eBook conversion by Emma Strong, San Diego, California

Dedication

To everyone in search of more...

This book is your unapologetic kick in the butt.

To be an unforgettable positive force in your world, a POI, it's imperative to expand your **will, work** and **wonder**. These 12 strategies will accelerate that journey.

Will, may your grit, determination, and drive be stirred in more deliberate ways.

Work, may your efforts and labor become more intentional and altruistic.

Wonder, may your impact on others be more auspicious and generative.

QR Codes

If you are unfamiliar, a QR Code or Quick Response Code is a two dimensional barcode that can be read using smartphone applications and dedicated QR reading devices. A QR code links directly to video, emails, websites, phone numbers, text and more.

You will find many QR codes in this book; so let's get started! Go to the App Store and download a QR reader. There are many to choose from, here are a few options:

Barcode Scanner

Zapper

NeoReader

Kaywa

freibergs.com
We want to hear from you at kevinandjackie@freibergs.com

jackiefreiberg

drjackiefreiberg

kevinfreiberg

kevinandjackie

Table of Contents

Okay isn't Okay

Look around you and look inside.
How many people do you think are settling? A lot!
People are settling into okay relationships
and okay jobs and an okay life.
And do you know why?
Because okay is comfortable.
Okay pays the bills, provides a warm bed at night,
and co-workers to have happy hour
with on Fridays.
But you know what okay is not?
Okay is not thrilling, it isn't passion,
it isn't a reason to go to bed late or
wake up early. Okay isn't life changing, fulfilling
and unforgettable.
Okay is not the reason you think big,
act bold, make a difference, and have an impact.

Don't settle, be strategic,
be mindful, be intentional, be a POI.
#poi #personofimpact

 People of Impact...

This book is designed to remind you that you are a POI—Person Of Impact. And you have a Pocket Of Influence.

Impact is about WHAT you do, HOW you do it and WHO you are. Your Impact is your reputation, your brand.

Dare to ask, dare to stretch, dare to grow, dare to think big and act bold! This book serves as a complement to a live keynote/workshop we deliver for leaders all over the country. We share it in written format for three reasons.

First, you cannot possibly remember all you hear in a workshop so this is a written reminder of the content delivered live.

Second, this book serves as an accountability buddy to help you continue your branding journey long after the workshop is complete.

Third, if you have not been a part of our POI workshop and would like to reimagine your brand, this book will serve as your Sherpa.

Person of Impact

Three simple letters. Three simple words that could change you, your life,
your family, your organization and your legacy.
#poi #personofimpact

POI | The difference between those who wait for permission and those who initiate.

POI | The difference between those who are controlled by fear and those who dare to try.

POI | The difference between those who procrastinate and those who get things done.

POI | The difference between those who allow feedback to buckle them and those who use it to grow.

POI | The difference between those who moan and those who move.

POI | The difference between those who use feedback as a weapon and those who use it as a gift.

POI | The difference between those who are distracted and those who are focused.

POI | The difference between those who harbor anger and those who shake it off.

POI | The difference between those who engage with arrogance and those who engage with humility.

POI | The difference between those who lead with fear and those who lead with love.

Well, sing, sing at the top of your voice,
Love without fear in your heart.
Feel, feel like you still have a choice
If we all light up we can scare away the dark

We wish our weekdays away
Spend our weekends in bed
Drink ourselves stupid
And work ourselves dead
And all just because that's what mom and dad said we should do

We should run through the forest
We should swim in the streams
We should laugh, we should cry,
We should love, we should dream
We should stare at the stars and not just the screens
You should hear what I'm saying and know what it means

To sing, sing at the top of your voice,
Love without fear in your heart.
Feel, feel like you still have a choice
If we all light up we can scare away the dark

Well, we wish we were happier, thinner and fitter,
We wish we weren't losers and liars and quitters
We want something more not just nasty and bitter
We want something real not just hash tags and Twitter

It's the meaning of life and it's streamed live on YouTube
But I bet Gangnam Style will still get more views
We're scared of drowning, flying and shooters
But we're all slowly dying in front of flipping computers

So sing, sing at the top of your voice,
Oh, love without fear in your heart.
Can you feel, feel like you still have a choice
If we all light up we can scare away the dark

We agree with Passenger;
it's time to scare way the darkness!

 # New YOU

It's no secret we live in a society where busy is over glorified; yet in the larger scheme of life and work, busy doesn't seem to be all that fulfilling.

Look around. People are exhausted, empty and unfulfilled in spite of the busy lives we lead. We run from meeting to meeting, from event to event and from activity to activity. Many of us find ourselves superficially and halfheartedly engaging in all the socially appropriate salutations.

Who among us can't identify with some version or another of this exchange?

"Hi! How are you? It's been too long."

"I know it sure has. We've been so busy. Life is crazy right now. But it's all good."

What does an exchange like that really offer? Too many of us find ourselves racing mindlessly through life with nothing meaningful to share or show for it.

Passenger's song, "Scare Away the Darkness," is a wake-up call encouraging us to push through the "darkness" that results when we mindlessly let the busy and empty routine of life—schedules, pace, professional pressures, overwhelming negativity, unrealistic expectations and social trends—dictate our choices and leave us comatose and robotic.

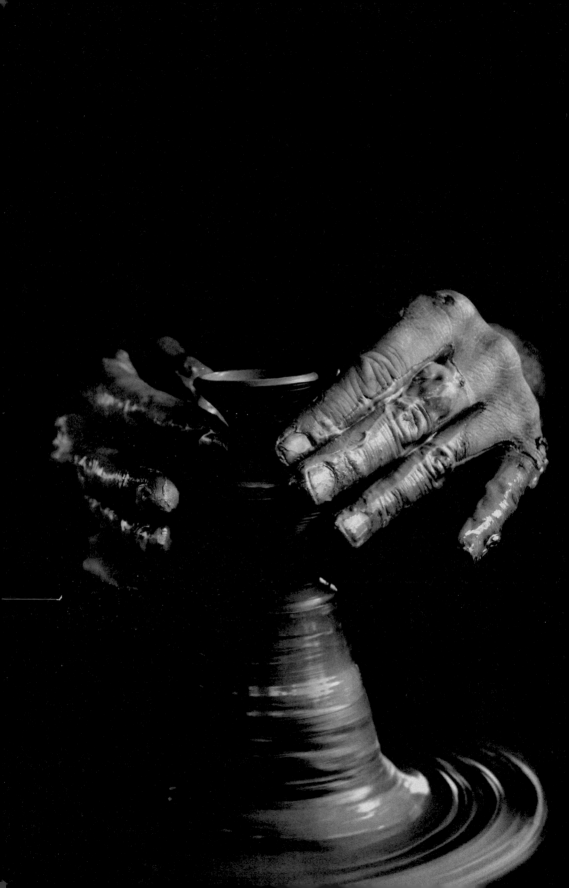

Your Future is in Your Hands

This book is a reminder that we have been designed to choose and we are defined by our choices.

You can reimagine, rethink, refresh, and even completely reengineer your brand and your life. Your life is in your hands.

The 12 POI strategies introduced in this book will help pave the way for you to start making intentional choices to scare away the darkness, step out of the mundane, stand out and be your best—one choice at a time.

Think of this as a 12-week experiment. Ideally, it is the beginning of a journey that challenges your habits, pushes your physical and mental boundaries and tests your beliefs. At times it may be difficult, frustrating, or even intimidating, but hopefully your victories will supersede your doubts.

Ideally, this is just the beginning of living your life more intentionally, purposefully and mindfully.

"When you realize that leadership is a choice, not a position or a title, the effect is liberating … or perhaps overwhelming. If it's liberating, you have the freedom to think big and act bold, to reimagine the leader you've become and the life you are living. You expand your impact and become a positive force for change. If it's overwhelming, don't give in! Keep this in mind, every moment of every day: You choose who you are and what you want to become. You get a second chance … every second."

— Jackie Freiberg

"POI is a serious wake-up call for every person who wants to change the cultural DNA of an organization stuck in doing business 'as usual' or a family stuck in the craze of a life overscheduled. This is no time to be a victim—it's time to exercise your freedom to choose, stand out and do extraordinary things!"

— Kevin Freiberg

At any given moment you have the power to say this is not how the story is going to end.

HOW ABOUT NOW?

#poi #personofimpact

12 POI Strategies to Redo You in 12 Weeks

This 12-week journey is designed to help you create a standout personal and professional brand. What if you could reprogram your mind, your behaviors and your habits to improve your impact? What if you could be free of the daily distractions that disrupt you from accomplishing things that matter and add value?

We think you can!

This can be a very personal journey; however, you will be far more successful if you lock arms and join a community of like-minded people who are also committed to lifelong brand building, people who are also growing, stretching, improving and developing.

Living with intention—physically, mentally and spiritually—is enriched and inspired by the community within which you are invested and connected. Ultimately you attract what you are. As you reimagine and rethink your brand and as you change your habits, choices and behaviors, you will attract more like-minded people. And, together, you will inspire others to do the same. This is a challenge and a commitment worthy of your time and attention.

Brand

Stepping out of the routine of business-as-usual to reconsider your impact and leadership brand is a valuable exercise if you want to improve your influence and impact both personally and professionally—to be the very best in your field.

What is a brand? Jeff Bezos is famous for saying, "It's what people say about you when you leave the room."

This will help you better understand what people are saying about you when you leave the room—it is a journey of self-awareness and leadership development.

Right now, among your colleagues, boss, clients, family and friends you have a brand—a reputation. Are you proud of that brand? Are there opportunities for improvement? Always!

Personal brand is what people say about you when you leave the room.

—Jeff Bezos, Founder Amazon.com

"Your smile is your logo, your personality is your business card, how you leave others feeling after an experience with you becomes your trademark."

We like to say, **"A brand is a promise of a pending experience."** It's your reputation! A Brand is your identity; it is what makes you unique—it's what makes you stand out. It precedes and follows you. Your brand defines you. According to Tom Peters in 2002, "A brand answers this question:

Who are you?"

What are you known for? Right now, you have a brand and in the context of YOU, it says to the world, when you deal with me here is what you can expect.

Try it...

What if you had to use only 144 characters to define you—your brand? What if you had to tweet your brand to the world? What would you tweet that is unique to you? Or to use Tom Peters' question, who are you?

A successful brand stands out in a sea of sameness; it establishes an identity. Successful brands are credible, trustworthy, respected and liked. Ideally, your brand makes you magnetic, someone people are drawn to.

When people think of you, do they feel a powerful connection? When people talk about you, what stories do they tell? Do they think of you as an unforgettable, get-it-done, go-to person; an industry expert, a thought leader, a guru who is indispensable and would be sorely missed if you ever left?

Every day we do things to either grow our brand equity or weaken it.

So what "promise of what pending experience" comes to mind for others when they anticipate working with you, talking with you, being in a meeting with you, or spending a day with you?

You can guess. And you can even hope that you know the right answer. Or you can ask.

What if you choose five people and ask them to share three words that describe your character, not you physically. Ask for the qualities that describe your character. This is about getting input on WHO you are, on WHAT you do, and on HOW you impact and influence others.

Be gutsy! Seek input from people who will give you honest and valuable input. Tell them why you are doing this and prepare yourself to hear things that may be difficult, but very helpful in creating a base from which you can challenge yourself to stretch, grow and rebuild.

"If you want to stand out from the crowd, give people a reason not to forget you."

–Richard Branson

Make a list of the characteristics you receive.

Are there any characteristics or qualities you want to change?

Each of us builds our brand through more than performance; we build our brand through character and character is built through words, gestures, signals and behaviors.

When people see you smile, is it a smile people are encouraged by, drawn to? When people encounter your personality, is it a personality people want to do business with? After spending time with you, do others feel drawn up, empowered, inspired, and energized? Or do people feel dragged down, heavy, disempowered, weak, and fearful?

Is your brand—that promise of that pending experience—a reputation, a trademark that you are proud of? Or is it a reputation you want to change? Regardless of your answer, this is what we know to be true...

The most important thing about you is not where you've been or the reputation, trademark or brand you've build to date. The most important thing about you is where you're headed and where you're going — the brand you WANT to build with intention and purpose.

If you were to build an unforgettable, we-can't-live-without-you, breakaway brand, what do you want to be known for?

It's time to reimagine your impact, your brand, your reputation, your trademark...

Before you fully commit to this 12-week challenge, review our 12 POI strategies and rate yourself on a scale of 1-5 (1 Low/5 High) for each strategy. Why not ask a few trusted friends to rate you as well. This will give you a benchmark on your base brand.

Let's get started.

12 POI Strategies

☐ I Self-Evaluate Weekly

☐ I List Goals Weekly

☐ I Keep Good Company

☐ I am a Connoisseur

☐ I Communicate Well

☐ I Manage My Mind

☐ I Say NO! I Get-It-Done

☐ I Enrich Lives

☐ I am Interested...And Interesting!

☐ I Exercise Daily

☐ I Practice the Art of the Apology

☐ I Forgive with Grace

KNOW GROW DRAW

Self-Evaluate Weekly

The journey toward improving your impact starts with a lifelong commitment to self-awareness and learning. Increasing self-awareness doesn't have to be a guru journey into the depths of your past. Self-awareness is having a clear perception of you—your personality, strengths, weaknesses, thoughts, beliefs, motivations, and emotions. Self-awareness also allows you to understand other people, how they perceive you, and how you respond to them in the moment, both behaviorally and emotionally.

It's typical to assume we are self-aware, but are we really? The ability to build a standout leadership brand, to be among the best in your space, requires you to create a state of heightened self-awareness.

Pay close attention to the details of your thoughts and behaviors. With practice we can learn to engage these types of heightened states and see new opportunities for interpretation of our thoughts, emotions and conversations.

> *Self-awareness is having a clear perception of you—your personality, strengths, weaknesses, thoughts, beliefs, motivations, and emotions.*

HOW? Think about these three words: Know, Grow and Draw.

Self-awareness allows us to see where our thoughts and emotions are taking us. It also allows us to KNOW and better understand what influences and controls our emotions, behavior and personality. Once we are aware, in the moment, of what influences our thoughts, emotions, words and behavior, then we have the ability to GROW, to make changes that will influence the direction of our brand, our lives.

By knowing ourselves, lifting off the blinders and being more self-aware, we can then grow by making adjustments and changing our behaviors to develop, stretch and improve ourselves.

Self-awareness is the first step in rethinking our brand and becoming what we want. It is about mastering our trademark, reputation; it's about reimagining our brand to be among the best.

Where we focus our attention, emotions, reactions, personality and behavior will determine our ability to have positive impact (or not).

Why Develop Self-Awareness?

As we develop self-awareness we are far better equipped to make adjustments in the thoughts and interpretations we make about the circumstances and people in our lives. Adjusting our interpretations and understanding of others allows us to better monitor and manage our attitudes and emotions. Self-awareness is one of many attributes influencing our Emotional Intelligence (EQ), which thanks to Daniel Goleman has been directly linked to leadership potential. In others words, strong leaders typically have strong EQ competencies; they are emotionally aware of self and the impact they have on others.

And it's through greater self-awareness and ongoing personal and professional growth that we earn the right to lead, to DRAW the best out of others.

Over the holiday season, lululemon promoted the "priceless" gift of presence vs. presents in their very popular social media campaign #TheGiftOfPresence, encouraging people to be present for each other as a priceless alternative to buying presents for each other!

Why? It's easy to get caught up in the routine of life, and if we are not careful, the routine of life can lull us into complacency. The routine of life can blind us to the opportunities around us and before we even realize it, the status quo becomes a new normal. "OK" becomes the enemy of better. Routine becomes the enemy of better or best. We settle into mediocrity. We settle into an acceptable brand at the expense of being a standout POI.

> *The routine of life can blind us to the opportunities around us before we even realize it.*

#poi #personofimpact

Sadly, we are in the midst of a global epidemic, an epidemic that threatens people in all parts of the world. The epidemic is Dead People Working™, people who robotically and routinely do what it takes to just get through the day. People who show up physically but are psychologically and emotionally checked-out. Dead people working are half-heartedly and half-headedly present at work and in life. To put it quite simply, they are not fully engaged.

Gallup measures employee engagement through their Q12 and sadly we are still struggling in our corporate attempts to raise engagement scores on a national and global level. The average company is … well, average, meaning 70% of people are either NOT engaged or actively disengaged at work and only 30% are fully engaged—checked in, passionate and fully present at work.

This must stop! We cannot allow this to become an acceptable "new" normal. Our dear friend Ken Blanchard likes to say "These are people who quit but they stay."

DEAD
PEOPLE
WORKING™

What about you? Are you living and operating like a DPW? Have you quit, but yet you continue to go through the motions at work, at home, in life?

- What part of you needs to step out of the routine and rethink, reimagine life fully engaged?
- What are you most passionate and excited about? What makes you come alive?
- What makes you NOT hit snooze and instead jump out of bed each morning?
- Where are the opportunities for you to make a difference and add value?
- What's your role in effecting a better future for you, for your family, and for your team, colleagues, and friends?
- What contribution will you commit to making each day?

You have to earn the right to DRAW the best out of others through your own personal and professional example. Re-thinking your brand means you need to invest the time to step out of the routine and self-evaluate.

Self-evaluation is an attempt to become more intentional about your behaviors, attitudes, contributions and impact. Self-evaluation leads to increased self-awareness.

Self-evaluation helps us lift off the blinders to better know, grow and strategically target areas to change and develop. Self-evaluation also paves the way for being more mindful and intentional about the impact we have on others.

> *"It's hard to get better at something if you don't reflect on it ... Without having that moment of self-evaluation, without that charge to improve on a daily or a weekly basis, you can't correct or change your behavior."*
> — Noah Weiss

As an example, take Noah Weiss, VP of Product Management at Foursquare. He fully understands the importance of self-awareness in his journey to be creative.

To stay focused on eliminating the frivolous distractions and to remain steadfast and focused on what adds value, Noah self-evaluates his creative output every week. And for additional accountability he posts his score online for his entire team to see. Weekly self-evaluation is how Noah steps out of the routine to seize the creative opportunities before him. This is how he drives growth, focus and contributions that add value.

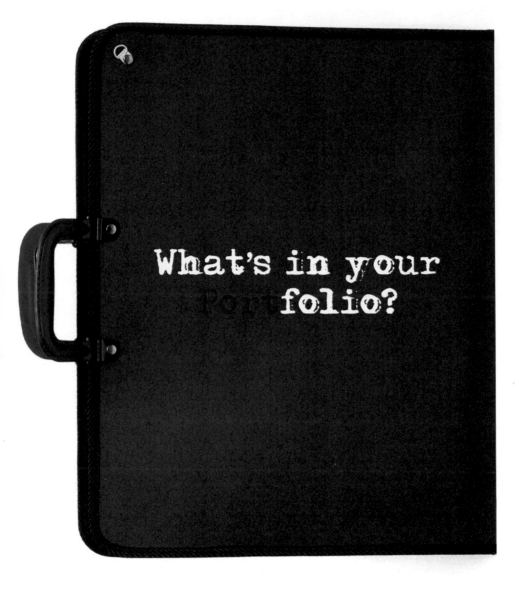

Over the last few years, we served as culture and leadership coaches to a very passionate leader of a Fortune 1000 insurance company. He too is committed to a weekly self-evaluation.

Every Sunday morning during his personal quiet time he engages in his own self-evaluation, but not on creativity alone. Instead, he evaluates himself on his success in living and leading what he has identified as the seven critical leadership skills: character, communication, courage, conviction, confidence, competence, and comprehension.

Every Sunday he reflects upon the previous week and then targets areas for improvement during the week ahead. Again, it is an intentional time of reflection that lifts the blinders and reveals opportunities for self-improvement.

The Value of Being Self-Aware

Think of an account executive from an ad agency being interviewed to make a pitch on a new account. It's the portfolio that counts! What are we saying? Who you've done work for, the level of creativity expressed in that work, the ROI of your campaign, your ideas—it all matters. Does your portfolio sell your brand, build your brand and draw others to want to work with you?

What if you had to reapply for your job every six months? You go in for your interview, open your portfolio and what's there? Stunning projects that shook the world or gave history a shove? What creative output are you responsible for and how has it added value? What leadership characteristics—creativity, communication, courage, conviction, confidence, competence, and comprehension—have helped you affect change and add value?

What did you wear on your first day... how about today?

Or, have work and life become routine, the same old thing? Not much is new, exciting or game changing!

Why not make a list of your projects over the last three years. What statement do they make about you? If you died tomorrow, would your project portfolio contribute to the legacy you want? To a reputation, a trademark you are proud of? If you're not happy with the answer, then it's time to redefine, reinvent and reimagine the project(s) you are currently working on or the one that's just around the corner.

People who have IMPACT never say, "Geez, nobody's given me anything interesting to work on lately."

It's your life! It's your career! It's your brand! If you want to be a stand out POI, you have to be willing and interested in going after the cool projects, and if there aren't any, create one.

It's your turn to lift off the blinders and become more self-aware.

Do you demand more from yourself than the organization demands from you? Not everyone can win, not everyone can be world-class, and not everyone can build a dynasty. Those who do, demand more from themselves.

If you truly want to improve your impact and be a highly regarded, best-in-class leader and well-respected person, are you worthy of that reputation?

Yes or No?

☐ ☐ Are you better prepared for a meeting or a phone call than anyone else?

☐ ☐ Do people applaud your sense of urgency and responsiveness?

☐ ☐ Do you take creativity and execution to a higher level?

☐ ☐ Are you constantly trying to get in your boss's head to figure out—strategically—where she is going next so you can be a significant player?

☐ ☐ Are you willing to take on projects no one else wants?

☐ ☐ When you meet a potential client for the first time do you know more about that person than any competitor will ever dream of knowing about them?

☐ ☐ Do you have a reputation for doing your homework?

☐ ☐ Do you go above and beyond?

How do you want to grow your IMPACT? What do you want to develop (GROW in yourself) AND what do you want to draw out of others (coach/mentor in others)?

What, how, and when will you self-evaluate to hold yourself accountable, improve self-awareness and steer your brand in an enlightened and a transformed direction?

SMART Goals

[S] Specific

[M] Measureable

[A] Achievable

[R] Realistic

[T] Time-bound

We are fond of saying, "Think Big, Act Bold." Thinking big requires us to dream big and acting bold requires us to do, as Nike advances, so shamelessly, "Just do it!" In other words, dare to try.

There are a lot of big dreamers out there, but dreaming without a plan or a deadline never amounts to much.

Realizing your goals requires you to be Dreamers AND Doers. How can you strive to be BOTH?

List your goals using the SMART goal template. It is a timeless practice. Why bother? Because SMART goals work, they make dreams doable.

It is easy to assume this is common knowledge and common practice. But, assumptions are not always accurate.

As an example, recently, after doing a keynote on POI, a very seasoned executive who leads an IT group in financial services approached us and said,

"Thank you for such a powerful reminder. I used to be very diligent and consistent in listing my goals. In looking back, it was very helpful in getting me to where I am today. But somehow, in the routine of life and the busy of business-as-usual, I got out of the habit. This reminded me of the value of dusting off that neglected but valuable habit. I'm committing to setting and achieving goals again."

DSN, DO SOMETHING NOW. Three simple letters and three simple words that can change your life and change the impact you can have in your organization and with your family.

The scarcest resource in organizations right now is not money, talent, ideas or power; it's people who DO, people who add value and get things done —people who dream AND do. Our book, *DO SOMETHING NOW!*, inspires Dreamers to become Doers.

What will it take to get you to set some SMART goals to become a standout POI?

Go for a walk, get some fresh air, find a place that frees you from distractions and dream … dream big. What big ideas come to mind? List your ideas, dreams and wishes.

Which of your dreams need to become goals with a SMART Plan?

Start with a list and end with a plan. Since the idea of listing and tracking "SMART" goals is timeless, listed below are 6 categories in which you may want to become more intentional and more planful. And if these categories don't resonate for you perhaps they will inspire other areas where you can become more goal-oriented, intentional and smart.

Career
— What level do you want to reach in your career, or what do you want to achieve? Stop waiting for permission! Be open to change. Step through fear.

Attitude
— Is any part of your mindset holding you back? If you always play it safe (make the right decision and take the politically correct road, the one most people take), you'll be just like everyone else. Acceptable, but plain, predictable, and perhaps boring ... Why not try something unique, stand out ... dare to try!

Education
— Is there any knowledge you want to acquire? What information and skills will you need to have in order to achieve other goals? What would you do today if you weren't afraid of making a mistake, feeling rejected, looking foolish? Knowledge isn't power until you DSN.

> *A goal without a plan is just a wish.*

Physical
— Are there any fitness goals that you want to achieve? Do you want good health for all of your life? What steps are you going to take to achieve these goals?

Pleasure
— How do you want to enjoy yourself more? We're fond of a popular quote that says, "If you're not living on the edge, you're taking up too much space!" What passion, hobby or talent have you tabled, pushed aside? Now is the time to revisit that passion or rekindle that hobby.

Community Service
— Do you want to make the world a better place? If so, how? What calls you? What community needs could benefit from you, your talents, and your time? Why not challenge yourself to serve a cause you're excited about?

Spend some time brainstorming these things and then select one or more goals that best reflect what you want to do.

Now Get "SMART" about creating a written plan to grow your Brand, improve your trademark and improve your impact—POI.

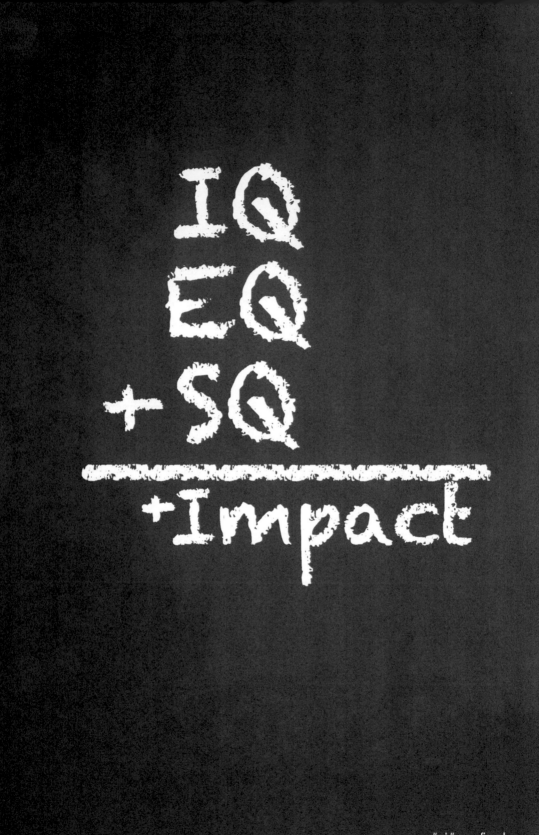

Week 3
Keep Good Company

In a world of increasing specialization and complexity, who you know becomes very important. The key isn't having all the answers. These days, the key to success is knowing who to go to for the right answers.

How many new people have you added to your contacts in the last six months? How many of those people have you reconnected with since you first met?

Being connected is also about tapping into various sources of knowledge (journals, people, competitors' annual reports, conferences, podcasts, books, blogs, TED Talks, websites, etc.) that help establish you as a connoisseur, a guru and/or a junction box for knowledge.

We have three children and we remind them (and ourselves) weekly that you're known by the company you keep, and that company (your friends, colleagues, your network) will drag you down or draw you UP!

You are only as cool, stimulating, adventurous, thoughtful, reflective, spiritual, or disciplined (you get the point) as the people you associate with. What's the collective IQ, EQ, SQ or any other "Q" of the gang you hang with? How big of a net do you cast? Do you go to lunch with the same people all the time? Or do you opt for a quiet working lunch at your desk, all on your own? Do you attend the same conferences with the same people?

Keeping good company and adding new connections requires changing your habits.

> *To keep good company, you must earn it. Again, you attract what you are.*

Why not do something to broaden your network and surround yourself with people who will stretch you in new directions—people who are different and fun and who bring something innovative and fresh to your network.

By the way, the key to this is being the kind of person cool people want to hang out with!

We have a saying in our home, "In all circumstances you have a choice; you can choose to behave or respond like a gentleman or a jerk, you can choose to be catty or classy." Your choice will impact your reputation and your brand, so be very intentional and choose carefully. We advocate gentleman and classy!

Brené Brown is a gifted researcher, author and speaker. Her TED Talks on Shame and Vulnerability are among the most viewed to date. In her book *Daring Greatly*, she noted that our generation is more in debt, overweight, out of shape, addicted and medicated than ever before in history.

Why?

We are empty! We are longing for more. One of our deepest human desires is to engage and connect, to be in meaningful relationships. Yet, we as a society have overglorified busy; we rush from one meeting, event, or activity to another.

It seems that busy is the new cool! To have no time on your calendar makes you important. Perhaps important, in demand and scheduled, but busy can be empty.

Our overly busy lives have shifted our focus from visiting, relaxing and engaging to rushing, stressing and overextending.

Kevin grew up in Rapid City, South Dakota and thankfully it is still a place where people make time to "visit." Visiting is socializing, relaxing and engaging with people while having meaningful and authentic conversations.

Rushing, stressing and overextending allow no time for this treasured and priceless activity, yet our spirit longs for it. We are wired for it. But, with this global glorification of busy, we have let relationships slip, which leaves a void—a void that needs to be filled.

Sadly, we look to fill the void with our own versions of pleasure and we find ourselves lost in our own private addictions.

WARNING

These addictions do not discriminate on the basis of age, gender, income or education; we are all vulnerable. So in an effort to fill the void, the emptiness, we get lost in a trashy novel, we watch mindless TV, or we go online and Facebook, instagram, snapchat and pin all night long. Or worse, we over pour, over eat, over shop and over medicate for a temporary pleasure to dull the pain and fill the void!

#poi #personofimpact

WHAT'S AT THE HEART OF YOUR SPENDING?

So how do we break this vicious cycle? How do we lean into something healthy and enriching instead of busy and empty? Self-reflect! How we spend our time and money says a lot about what we value. Be more intentional about how you spend your money and your time. Take a close and critical look at your checkbook and your calendar.

Then ask yourself:

- Am I proud of how I spend my time?

- What adjustments do I need to make?

- Am I as focused and present as I should be, or am I distracted by the pace and demands of my schedule?

- Am I spending my money on things that are enriching my life? Or am I stufficating (an addiction to stuff, materialism and having more than I need).

- Do I have more stuff than I have friends, family, community, or meaning in my life?

Recently, we hosted an executive retreat at our home in Sundance and one of the executives made a simple yet powerful point about how she and her daughter had committed to "making memories," doing cool things and creating experiences together instead of going shopping together. They choose to spend money on memories, not things. Things perish. Memories last a lifetime—they're priceless and timeless.

STOP the Gloirication of Busy

How you choose to spend your time and money will define you. What's more exciting—taking an inventory of all your stuff and telling your friends and associates about it? Or is it more exciting and meaningful to relive and share your experiences, travels and adventures—events and experiences that have shaped and defined you?

We too are consciously choosing to spend our time and money on enriching experiences and we are trying to unstufficate.

How can you be more intentional about keeping good company? Do the people you spend the majority of your time with draw you up (make you better)? Are they engaging in enriching activities, experiences and adventures? Are you better because they are in your life? And are they better because you are in theirs?

EVALUATE THE PEOPLE IN YOUR LIFE ; THEN PROMOTE, DEMOTE, OR TERMINATE. YOU'RE THE CEO OF YOUR LIFE.

Here are some pointed questions.

- What are your conversations about?
- What you do? What you want to do?
- Are you talking about your challenges, mistakes, fears, dreams and desires?
- Or are you talking about what you have, about your stuff?
- Who do you need to spend more time with?
- Who drags you down? With whom do you need to limit your time?

Make a personal and professional list and do something to grow a healthy, enriching community every day. It's what we all crave.

Busy really shouldn't be the new cool. Being in a rush doesn't have to be fashionable. And, having NO time for the priceless things in life, well… it's just wrong.

Here are 10 life practices to live by:

1. **Live for a legacy:** What do you want to be known for? Is it a fancy office, big house, cool car, stuff? Or is it the love and respect of family and friends? Not that these things are mutually exclusive, in fact they shouldn't be. We're committed to faith, family, friends and achieving great fruits for our labor, but fruit comes in all kinds of things, not just stuff. We've discovered greater fulfillment through making time to visit and growing our relationships—leaning into great business partnerships, giving back to our community, and spending time with family and treasured friends.

2. **Keep calm:** Avoid stress. Although stress may be an adrenaline rush for some of us, research shows that it is far more harmful than it is good. Avoid it, shake it off, and sweat it out. Why? Because research proves that stress, over the long term, is damaging to your health and well-being.

3. **Be well:** Become the very best keeper of your body; it's the only one you have. Eat intentionally, drink more water, do some kind of exercise every day, and replenish and recover with a good night's sleep. Eat, move and sleep mindfully. Get a Fitbit or a Jawbone to monitor your movement and sleep patterns. Once you start measuring and monitoring your movement and sleep, you will be more purposeful and mindful about your activity. (Much more on this in Strategy #10)

4. **Unplug:** If we're honest, we all have ADD (Addiction to Digital Devices). Engage in a 30-day challenge (or whatever time frame is doable/achievable for you). Identify a no screen zone (at dinner, on Sunday, during a workout) and find time to talk, daydream, and reflect—without technology. Unplug and refresh! For inspiration watch Matt Cutt's TED Talk (simply scan the QR code on page 48).

5. **Stretch your mind:** Be a lifelong learner. Read, learn, or try something totally new and different, and then talk about it or share it and spread the passion. Jackie stretches in all directions and the joke in our family is she thinks she has a PhD in everything! For the family it's funny, but in the bigger scheme of things she is very diversified in her reading and she is committed to being able to hold a conversation in a variety of unrelated areas.

6. **Trust your gut:** When we're busy we don't have time to listen to the sixth sense or that gut feel. Slow down, give yourself a chance to think, reflect and go with your gut. Walk, drive, or talk to a trusted friend and insights will come to mind.

7. **Play:** Jackie's dad was a very successful executive in financial services and he was passionate about saying, "It's easier to work hard if you play hard too." We agree! Find some fun activities to indulge in. Let loose and have fun.

8. **Professionalism and seriousness:** are highly overrated! Innovations and creative ideas are often inspired by a change in perspective and a fresh outlook. Commit to time for play; it will improve your work performance and it may even improve your network.

9. **Serve:** A busy, overscheduled life leaves little room for serving others. Think about your talents, gifts and passions. Share them and give them freely; you will gain immeasurable joy, enrich the lives of others and grow your connections.

10. **Practice gratitude:** Before the craze of the day sets in, find a quiet space and think of at least three things to be grateful for all day and keep them top of mind. And, why not capture your thoughts in a gratitude journal? A grateful mindset inspires optimism, hope and happiness, all of which are contagious so other like—minded people will be drawn to you.

Review and rethink

Do you value your money and your time? If so, a review of how you spend your money and your time is always insightful. Busy can lead to convenient, wasteful spending and frivolous uses of time. Ask yourself this question, "Am I spending my time and money on what I value?" If not, reset and adjust.

Keeping good company requires us to slow down, smell the roses, sip our coffee, take long walks and make the time for some good old fashion "visits."

JEFF BRIDGES · MAGGIE GYLLENHAAL

CRAZY HEART

FOX SEARCHLIGHT PICTURES PRESENTS AN INFORMANT MEDIA / BUTCHERS RUN FILMS PRODUCTION JEFF BRIDGES MAGGIE GYLLENHAAL "CRAZY HEART" ROBERT DUVALL
STEPHEN BRUTON AND T BONE BURNETT DOUG HALL JOHN AXELRAD WALDEMAR KALINOWSKI BARRY MARKOWITZ A.S.C. JEFF BRIDGES
MICHAEL A. SIMPSON ERIC BRENNER LESLIE BELZBERG ROBERT DUVALL ROB CARLINER JUDY CAIRO T BONE BURNETT THOMAS COBB SCOTT COOPER

Become a Connoisseur

Eric Hoffer is famous for saying, "In times of drastic change it is the learners who will inherit the future. The learned find themselves equipped to live in a world that no longer exists."

Are you constantly learning? Or have you arrived?

Our friend and one of the most respected leaders in the world, Herb Kelleher, Founder and Chairman Emeritus of Southwest Airlines, is fond of saying, "At the height of our success we are most vulnerable to complacency."

On a similar note, when Synovus Financial was recognized as the #1 Best Company to Work for In America, their Chairman Jimmy Blanchard, another friend and respected leader, said at their corporate celebration, "YES! We are great today! And we must be better tomorrow."

What are all these iconic leaders saying? Success is a journey. We can never rest on yesterday's headline, for that is what the learned do, they assume they have arrived and then settle for too long.

Think back to the 2009 film, Crazy Heart, a very dark but poignant example of resting on yesterday's headline. Jeff Bridges earned the 2009 Best Actor Award for his performance as "Bad" Blake, a 57-year old alcoholic, has-been singer/songwriter. Bad, once a very successful country music star and headliner, now finds himself playing in small town bars and on the rare occasion as backup for the new young stars.

Most days he's staying in dive hotels and drinking his misery away. His life seems to turn when a young journalist, played by Maggie Gyllenhaal, on a quest for a story requests an interview. She remembers Bad from his days of fame.

On the morning she arrives for the interview, Bad is hung over, humbled and apologetic. Just as Gyllenhaal is about to begin the interview, Bad interrupts her and says, "I feel obligated to apologize for being less than you imagined me to be."

So what does this have to do with becoming a connoisseur? A connoisseur never rests on yesterday's headline. A connoisseur is recognized as an authority.

In time of change, learners inherit the earth...while the learned find themselves beautifully equipped to deal with a world that no longer exists.

–Eric Hoffer

Connoisseurs are relentless in their quest for knowledge. Bad lost his edge and stopped trying. He gave up on his passion and rested for too long on a headline that quickly faded while others surpassed him.

Going back to the advice of Hoffer, Kelleher and Blanchard, connoisseurs are lifelong learners, and they do not allow success to slow their quest for better.

Think about a connoisseur of fine wine. A connoisseur can tell you what's new in the industry, what grape growers are doing, what's grown in a certain region, which harvests are particularly good, where to source hard-to-find vintages, what are the nuances of hosting a tasting and the best food pairings, how to get on the lists of exclusive wineries, etc. And, every time you talk to a connoisseur, he or she will bring something new to the discussion.

- Do you bring this kind of value to your team, your business, and your family?

- Do you have a reputation for being a connoisseur in your field?

- Can you document what you've learned in the last three weeks that will add value to your company?

- In the last three months have you connected with three new people who could help you grow your business or improve your impact?

- Has your arsenal of skills expanded in the last three months?

- Has your contribution to your company in the last three months been worth bragging about?

Think about it, every day people around us are getting better, technology is advancing, information is exploding and customers are getting smarter and more demanding. If the organization or the world we live in is changing faster or learning more than we are, then we have a problem.

Remember, every meeting, every project and every conversation is a statement about you; make them matter.

Between the two of us we give 80-some presentations a year. Every one of them counts. We build our brand one research call, one program, and one keynote at a time. Kevin's in Dallas, Jackie's in Denver—both making 75 minute presentations to 500 audience members. That's precious little time to make a mark, but to do so, we bring every ounce of energy we have to the game because we want to enrich lives and we want to grow businesses. 75 minutes—rock the world or crash and burn. Our keynotes, our books and our executive coaching are our signature, our opportunity to create a masterpiece. What's yours?

LIMITATIONS DO NOT HAVE TO BE LIMITING.

Now, you. How many things are you working on RIGHT NOW that will be remembered by others five years from now? Life, meaning, and passion come from working on things that turn you on—things that make your pride soar! Stagnant water is dead.

When we submit ourselves to the same old boring, routine, mundane crap, we die a little bit each day. Death is only one of the ways we lose our lives. This is precisely why there are so many dead people working. Look, you're going to die. But, don't you want to LIVE first?

Unless your organization is an exception to the rule, you live in what our friend and venture capitalist Billy Glynn calls an intellectual desert. This doesn't mean you don't work with really smart people; it means there is a drought of ideas. People who consistently come up with new ideas are a rare breed.

Idea generators make people think, keep things fresh, and generate more ideas. People with ideas demonstrate that they are thinking about the business and about growth. What was the last idea you planted on the table? Why is this so important? The business world is full of uncertainty and few people will give you enough money, resources, time or color-by-number directions to get a job done. But, we all put our faith in those who have the grit, drive, hunger and confidence to find a way—those who aren't turned off by do-more-with-less and those who aren't

> *When we submit ourselves to the same old boring, routine, mundane crap, we die a little bit each day.*

afraid to be adventurous. In most big companies, unlimited resources foster bloat, waste and complacency. Limitations do not have to be limiting. If we dare to think big and act bold—if we dare to try—limitations have the power to inspire creativity, cost savings, improved efficiencies and service enhancements.

Routine and success can be blinding. Connoisseurs and lifelong learners live alert; they are wide awake to their surroundings and they do not allow routine to become white noise that blinds them to possibility and innovations.

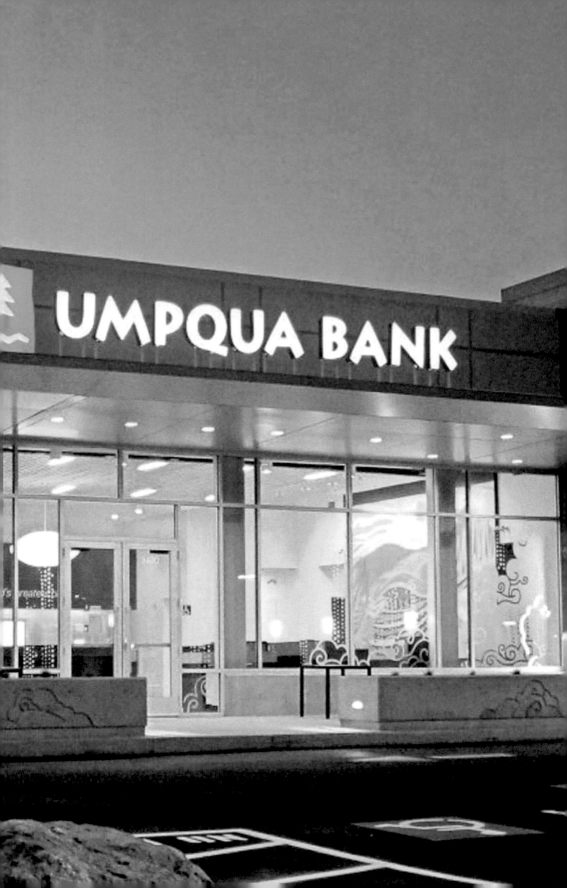

The big idea here is never stop learning. What do you want to be known as an expert in?

Connoisseurs are always a step ahead; they are creating the tipping points.

How do you invite and challenge people to discover, innovate and see the possibilities before them? How do you inspire your people to look beyond work and to see beyond their daily routines?

Umpqua Bank is one of the most successful independent banks in the U.S. and they work on it diligently.

To inspire ongoing learning and to generate fresh ideas all in the spirit of enhancing banking services, Umpqua encourages and hosts mission trips.

For Umpqua, their competition is not other financial services firms; they consider other retailers as their best competitors. So to stay in the know and to encourage associates to be alert, to be fully aware and to borrow from the best, Umpqua Bank associates visit other retailers. Their primary mission is to find an idea to implement at Umpqua.

This encourages lifelong learning and it empowers, enables and engages people to "Dare to Try."

People are NOT our most valuable assets. Today, ideas are our most valuable assets. Innovation in its simplest form is the result of people bringing ideas to life. Yet, research shows 52% of employees are frustrated at work because managers do not support their ideas or empower their creativity. People who present ideas often get no response at all from a supervisor (the idea goes into a black hole). Or they get responses like these:

"No, that won't work." "No, we've already tried that." "No, we do it this way." "No, our customers won't like that." "No, that's not realistic." "No, they will never buy into that." "No, we can't afford that."

We don't buy the assumption that managers aren't interested. Instead, we suggest that you think through why they are not responding or why they are so quick to say "NO."

Could the reasons be any versions of the following?

Your manager, partner, or colleague doesn't understand, doesn't see the ROI, is insecure and unsure of the future, is overwhelmed in his/her own role, or is distracted by other issues.

Regardless of the scenario, it is up to us to take personal responsibility for our ideas and build a business case for the ROI of an idea.

WE AIN'T NO

...FACE SAVIN,
...EXCUSE MAKIN,
...RULE FOLLOWIN,
...FUN SQUELCHIN,
...PERMISSION SEEKIN,
...STATUS QUO PROTECTIN,

CLOCK PUNCHIN, BUREAUCRATS
WE'RE RISK TAKERS, TRAIL BLAZERS,
RULE BREAKERS AND
REVOLUTIONARIES

WE MAKE A DIFFERENCE!

#poi #personofimpact

Here are 6 strategies you can use to bring your idea to life:

Make it practical. Ideas can be vague. Show examples, create a prototype and get customer input on the viability of your idea. Make your idea visual. To see is to believe! Need inspiration? Order our book *DO SOMETHING NOW!*

Show customer benefit. Capture customer concerns, frustrations and suggestions. Show how your idea/innovation will provide a solution. Get customers to buy into a trial or a focus group dedicated to your idea and document their experiences.

Find co-partners or collaborators. Innovations are challenging, look for possible partners to co-develop your idea. If it's too complex for your own organization or your team to tackle on your own, do your research and get to know the subject matter experts in other functional areas. Reach across functional boundaries, tap into the talents of others. You will likely grow your knowledge, network and reputation in the process.

Invite your manager, a colleague or a partner to co-own the initiative. Innovations are typically team efforts that are best led by passionate innovation co-champions, co-sponsors, or co-owners. You do the work but give your manager co-credit.

Supporting and accelerating an idea through a deeply rooted corporate culture often requires a team of champions…collaborate.

Build a business case for your idea. As an innovator, a connoisseur, your idea must always offer ROI. Show how your idea reduces costs, improves a process, increases efficiency, adds more value than costs, builds your brand, decreases turnover, increases retention, or helps your team achieve goals/objectives.

Choose the right time to introduce your idea. Timing is everything. Prepare don't just share! Just because the idea is top of mind for you doesn't mean it is timely for everyone else. Once you've created a business case for the ROI, have identified go-to resources and possible collaborators, gained customer input, and linked your idea to the goals of the organization or your family, then you can carefully think through when and how to share it. Make the idea timely and timeless. Schedule a time to share your business case when others can be focused and distractions are minimized.

People want to add value and contribute; people want to become connoisseurs!

- What are you learning? And are you considered a connoisseur?
- How are you inspiring others to learn?
- Are you building a business case and sharing your ideas appropriately?
- Are you equipping people with the tools and strategies they need to bring their ideas to life?

Week 5
Communicate Well

One day on morning radio, the hosts were inviting listeners to call in with their favorite catch phrase—any phrase or expression recognized by its repeated utterance.

This was our favorite, Say what you mean, mean what you say, never say it mean!

Remember the saying back when we were kids, "Sticks and stones will break my bones but names will never hurt me." Well who ever came up with that was WRONG! Calling people names and using harmful words is mean and is better known today as bullying. And bullying doesn't just happen to kids at school; bullying happens in businesses and yes, it even happens in the home as well.

Your words can be your greatest gifts or your most destructive weapons. Words and tone provide a window into your brand, your vision, your values and your ability to engage and inspire others. Change your words … change your behaviors, your brand and your world.

Herb Kelleher again, the Founder, Chairman Emeritus of Southwest Airlines, is famous for saying, "It is okay to be tough, but not mean." In other words, as leaders, parents, and friends, there will be times when we need to deliver tough, uncomfortable truths to others. Yet, great leaders who understand the power of words and tone are never abrupt, impatient, mean or bully-like in their delivery of tough truths.

> *Your words can be your greatest gifts or your most destructive weapons.*
>
> #poi #personofimpact

To get better at **"say what you mean, mean what you say, don't say it mean,"** we have to be willing to practice! Think about delivering tough truths to help, not hurt people. Difficult feedback can and should be delivered in the spirit of revealing the truth to increase self-awareness and help others change, grow, learn and improve. Delivering difficult feedback is not about blindsiding, insulting or hurting another person.

Gifted leaders understand the power of communication and regard it as a valuable skill. What you say (the words you use) and how you say or share your words will influence your brand, both positively and negatively.

So, whether you are running a company, leading a team, or managing a family, here are 7 things gifted leaders say and do often to communicate more effectively and draw the best out of others.

1. Here's our plan.

Lead with vision. Share a picture of the results you want to create. People will offer great suggestions if they understand the bigger picture. People appreciate a direct line of sight. Once people understand the where and why, then they can help define the how. A clear vision will also keep people focused and on track. And clarity gives everyone the confidence to say "no" to things inconsistent with achieving your vision. Even kids need to be a part of a bigger vision. Practice sharing things like, "Mom has to work until 4 p.m. and then we can go for a walk and start dinner together."

2. What do you need?

People need to know that you care about them personally and professionally and that you want them to succeed. Once you share the vision then it's important for you to leverage every person. Servant leaders help pave the way for others to stretch, grow and develop. Again, kids need this too. "After school it's important to take a play break, have a healthy snack, and then settle in to do your homework." It's easier to work hard when you have some time to play hard too.

3. Tell me more.

Ask for input and listen to understand. Let people know you're interested in their ideas. Give others implicit permission to share their opinions. Then, zip it! Staying quiet, even if it's uncomfortable, invites others to engage and offer their ideas and insights.

4. Way to live our values!

Celebrate and recognize people who live the company's values. When people use these values to make good business decisions, engage in servant leader behaviors to add value to others then let them know you noticed. Make your values a part of your everyday conversation. It's not always easy to celebrate some values. Suppose one of your corporate values is "invite difference of opinion." If someone on your team disagrees with you and shares a difference of opinion, do you celebrate their willingness to live the value or do you walk away frustrated and determined to help them see it your way? Do you covertly write them off, stop asking, stop including, and stop showing interest? Do a reality check here. How do you coach and communicate around any value that inspires a potential difference of opinion? Are you OK to agree to disagree?

5. You can count on me.

Your team needs to trust you. So let them know, frequently, that you've got their back. Then, you need to work like heck to prove it and deliver on your promises. While writing NUTS!, we remembered a story of how Herb Kelleher responded to a letter from an irritated customer who happened to catch a Southwest Airlines flight attendant mooning a colleague on a flight. Herb wrote back saying, "We're sorry you caught us with our pants down!"

ELEVATE COOPERATION AND COLLABORTION TO AN ART FORM.

BE ACCOUNTABLE

6. We can do better.

Good isn't always good enough! Never let good get in the way of better. Celebrate people when they do well, but always be willing to coach people when they don't achieve their potential. And always be an example. Don't be afraid to lead by example, admit your mistakes and share your development plan—model self-awareness and change.

7. Let's celebrate!

Be careful. Do not create a culture in which the only reward for great work is MORE work. Instead, make it a habit to celebrate wins (big and small). People are much more willing to work hard if they are given the opportunity to play hard too. As a team come up with some inexpensive and meaningful ways to celebrate your wins and offer inspirational shout outs to people who have earned them. Let the team decide how to celebrate and let them own/ champion how and when to do the celebrating.

Being an intentional communicator is a skill that always needs to be refined. It is an art and a science. To be sure your message is received as you intend it to be, it is best to put yourself in the shoes of the receiver.

Think about what you know about the person. What is the best way to share information with them? Are they a bottom line, get-to-the-point kind of person? Or do they need details and specific examples? Are they highly relational and will they need some reassurance?

Communication is not sender-based, it is receiver-based. Craft your message with the recipient in mind. Are you blunt and abrupt, and do you expect people to see your message as in their best interests? In other words, do you expect them to listen, suck it up and get over it? If so, your brand will suffer. We are not advocating being a pushover; we're advocating being tough, just not mean-spirited. You can be tough and honorable to the communication needs of others—it requires a keen sense of self-awareness and empathy to the needs of others.

And when in doubt, strive for simplicity. Our lives are already busy and chaotic, so avoid complicated messages. Typically, if your message is complicated then you are confused. Practice, simplify and be kind. And never "hint and hope." In other words, do not beat around the bush and think others will understand.

Communication can also get very confused when we make assumptions. Try not to take everyone in your life personally; everyone has a story behind their behaviors.

"Could a greater miracle take place than for us to look through each other's eyes for an instant?"

-Henry David Thoreau

There is always a story behind the story. Try practicing empathy or asking before you judge. This Cleveland Clinic video went viral. It is a very emotional example of personal struggle and its impact on our behavior.

Great communicators strive for simplicity in their messages and always seek first to understand before making assumptions.

- Who in your life would benefit if you simplify your messages?

- Who would benefit if you ask more questions?

- Who would benefit if you show more empathy?

- Who needs you to extend more grace?

By answering these questions and changing your approach you will build a brand that is less about reacting to others and more about being a positive influence on others.

empathy —
the ability to understand and share the feelings of another

sympathy —
o understanding between ppl, common feelings
o support in the form of shared feelings or opinions

Week 6
Manage Your Mind

We manage people, budgets, time, assets, and even our weight. What about our minds?

It is really important that we sanctify our minds and our imaginations because our thoughts influence our behaviors, our emotions and in turn our futures.

Nike understands the power of pushing through a mental mindset that will hold you back. Allowing a lifestyle of negativity to become permanent and pervasive will eventually suck the life out of you and everyone around you, literally and figuratively.

Even though you might be tired, lean into the Nike motto, JUST DO IT! Some people are eternal optimists and they see the world as abundant, plentiful and hopeful. In contrast, there are others who are die-hard pessimists, who see the world as scarce, limited and threatening.

Dr. Martin Seligman is a prolific author, researcher and thought leader in the area of learned optimism. Known as the father of the new science of positive psychology, Seligman draws on more than 20 years of clinical research to

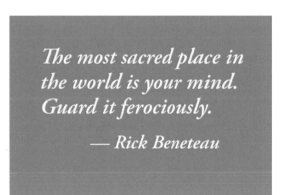

The most sacred place in the world is your mind. Guard it ferociously.

— Rick Beneteau

demonstrate how optimism enhances the quality of life and how anyone can learn to practice it. He offers many simple techniques and explains how to develop a more constructive explanatory style for interpreting our behaviors by engaging in a more positive (optimistic) internal dialogue.

There is significant proof that the practice of learned optimism can help control depression, boost our immune system, positively influence our potential, and make us happier.

Many people believe that "perception is reality." Maybe so, but is that reality accurate? Is it optimistic or pessimistic? Well, it depends on our internal dialogue and it depends on the internal agreements we have made with ourselves. Our mental agreements (our thoughts and interpretations) may not be accurate, but they sure do feel real!

In Dr. Seligman's book, *Learned Optimism*, he teaches us how to manage our minds to improve our lives. Or, more simply, how to change our thoughts so we can more positively influence our world.

To rewire your brain to be more optimistic and to improve performance, intelligence, energy and creativity try doing these 5 things every day for the next 21 days:

1. List 3 things you are grateful for each day.

2. Journal about one positive experience in your day.

3. Exercise (move—when dopamine flows through you good things happen physiologically, more on this in Exercise Daily, Strategy #10).

4. Pray or reflect (even if only for 10 minutes)… but before you start, eliminate distractions and turn off the digital devices.

5. Do one random act of kindness every day.

Research shows if we are positive in the present (aka happy) we are more optimistic. And research proves that being happy (positive in the present) helps us work harder, faster and smarter in all things.

Here is a very real time example of the power of managing our minds. In our consulting practice we work with professional baseball players and occasionally we've heard friends say, Wouldn't it be great to get paid millions to do what you love? No arguments there. But, remember there is always a story behind the story.

Under the leadership and coaching of Bruce Bochy, the San Francisco Giants have won three World Series Championships in five years. Bruce is a good friend and a phenomenal leader. We are always amazed at the emotional highs and lows he has to manage—particularly during the playoffs. Losing a critical game means facing the onslaught of a hostile and mocking media; dealing with frustrated fans, friends and family; handling the pressure from a front office that might question the decisions you made on the field; and making sure each player in the clubhouse is mentally and emotionally prepared to win the next game. It's an emotional roller coaster. Without the right temperament, you could lose your mind over 162 games.

Ultimate success requires the ability to bounce back. In business and in life, it's not that the winners don't have bad days, it's not that they don't experience defeat—it's that they are RESILIENT. They don't hit the panic button; they learn from a loss, let go and move on. How did you handle the last setback you experienced?

#poi #personofimpact

In 2013 the Giants went into the San Diego Padres series having lost 14 out of their last 16 games. Word on the street, in the media, on the field, in the clubhouse and in the players' heads was: "the Giants are in a FUNK!"

We worked with Bruce and designed a pre-game "Funk NO!" talk for all the players. We talked about how the voice of I Am NOT can take you out and create a very harmful mindset and an inaccurate but powerful perspective. We created black t-shirts printed with big bold orange "FUNK NO" across the front. In the dugout, you could hear the players chanting "Funk NO!"

That very afternoon, Tim Lincecum made baseball history again. He threw 148 pitches for a no-hitter San Francisco Giants win.

Be careful. Do not believe the lies of the world around you. People, the media, routine, and even shitty circumstances will plant lies into us. Harsh words, anger, betrayal, bad news, or an illness all have the power to bruise, wound and set us back. But through learned optimism and managing our minds we can develop more positive and constructive approaches for interpreting these events in our lives.

Shake it off!

We have an 80 pound golden retriever, named Romeo who loves the water. Think about the image of Romeo coming out of the water. What is his first instinct? To shake like crazy! Shed the extra weight, get rid of the water.

Perhaps that offers a good visual to keep top of mind. Why not shake off the lies, the setbacks, and the bad news? Shed the extra weight! Negative thoughts are toxic and believing the lies inspires pessimism; it's another form of cancer.

Manage your mind by practicing learned optimism. It is a behavior worth learning and practicing.

- What lies are you holding on to?
- What mental agreements have created a pessimistic perspective and need adjustments?
- What setbacks need a more positive frame?
- What bad news do you need to shed, shake off, let go of and move on from?

Follow
One
Course
Unitl
Sucessful

Say NO! Get-it-Done.

These days we all have ADD...We are Addicted to Digital Devices.

To rethink, reimagine, refresh or even reengineer your brand, you will need to eliminate the distractions and focus. Are you willing to say NO to frivolous distractions?

Research shows we are either other or self-interrupted every 3 minutes. And, on average, it takes 23 minutes to refocus. With those kinds of numbers how will we ever catch up?

To compound the problem, the research also proves that 80% of our interruptions are trivial (frivolous) or perhaps important to someone else, but not to us. Yet we get caught up in their importance and neglect our own priorities. Or we do what is convenient, not necessarily what is adding value, generating revenue or inspiring innovations. Instead we do the urgent but unimportant. It's time to FOCUS - Follow One Course Until Successful.

But how? Here are two simple and very doable ideas for enhancing focus:

Manage caffeine. Although we may think caffeine helps us focus, the opposite may be true. Caffeine can stay in our systems for more than 12 hours. Try to skip caffeine in the afternoon and evening. It triggers the release of adrenaline and ignites the "fight-or-flight" response. Too much caffeine puts your brain and body into a hyper-aroused state of stress and your emotions overrun your behavior. The fight-or-flight mechanism sidesteps rational thinking in favor of a faster response. This is beneficial when a bear is chasing us, but not when we're responding to a blunt email. The stress that caffeine creates is far from intermittent. Caffeine takes its sweet time working its way out of our bodies so the stress it creates is, more often, prolonged (which is more harmful than helpful).

Manage sleep. Self-control, attention, focus and memory are all reduced when you don't get enough—or the right kind of—sleep. Sleep deprivation raises stress hormone levels, even without a stressor present. When you sleep, your brain literally recharges. It shuffles through the day's memories, storing or discarding them (aka dreams), so you wake up alert and clear-headed. Stressful projects often make you feel as if you have no time to sleep, yet sleep is exactly what you need to get things under control and to focus.

Strive for increasing the quality and quantity of your sleep. Starting on Monday, go to bed five minutes earlier than the night before. It won't feel like a huge change day-to-day, but by Friday you could be getting 30 more minutes of rest per night.

Here are a few more helpful sleep tips. Avoid tech gadgets an hour before bed. Try to keep your bedroom as dark as possible and the room temperature between 65-70 degrees F.

And if we still haven't convinced you of the value and importance of sleep, watch this TED Talk by Jeff Lliff on the link between sleep and Alzheimer's disease.

Focus is also improved when we have a bigger YES (a more important priority). A bigger YES gives us the confidence and freedom to say NO to the frivolous and unimportant distractions of life. And saying NO for a bigger YES is the key to developing a brand where you are known for your ability to focus and establish priorities to get things done.

People who GET-IT-DONE are usually very focused. Would people describe you as a get-it-done person?

Get-it-done people can distinguish between urgent and important, long-term value vs. short-term value, and dreaming vs. doing. They know that FOCUS is the result of making hard choices among these alternatives based on sufficient information. People who GET-IT-DONE are extremely disciplined when it comes to making sure that the priorities are understood, the distractions are minimized, and the plan is in place.

Initiative is an important bigger YES! Do you initiate projects on your own vs. playing the victim and hiding behind the veil of I don't know how to do it or I've never done that before. Taking initiative means you look for ways to cut costs or create new revenue streams without being asked. It means you build an aggressive marketing campaign to grow sales vs. waiting for the orders to come in. And, if you haven't got the slightest clue about how to do that, you surround yourself with a network of people who do and then learn like crazy. It means you volunteer for bigger, more challenging assignments.

Thriving brands are built on GUMPTION—the courage to take whatever action is needed. If you are afraid of making a mistake, being wrong, upsetting the chain of command or getting in over your head, you will never show much initiative.

Here are two more helpful tips for becoming a get-it-done POI by increasing your focus:

Say NO to endless meetings. People are experiencing meeting overload. It creates stress and stress, if prolonged, will lower our effectiveness.

Generally speaking, people tend to be most creative in the mornings between 8 a.m. and noon. Yet businesses are notorious for holding mandatory morning meetings.

People are rushing from one meeting to the next. If one meeting ends late, they bust into the next without any time for reflection or any time to be planful and proactive.

GOT A MEETING?
TAKE A WALK

More so than ever, people are complaining that they barely have time to accomplish their real jobs because they are too busy rushing from one meeting to another.

What is your life like? Are meetings and other frivolous distractions depleting your productivity? Are meetings getting in the way of your ability to focus?

What is your more important, bigger YES? What if you block out a few mornings a week to work on projects or simply schedule some creative time? Schedule as many meetings as possible in the afternoon and schedule them so you can walk and talk.

Say NO to sitting. Make walk and talk meetings a big, bold YES!

When you do have to sit, if there is no alternative, then we suggest you sit smart.

Slouching will zap your energy and your mood, and over time it can lead to muscle fatigue, pain and even long term injury. Straighten up by sitting toward the front of your chair with your hips titled slightly forward. Make sure both feet are hip width apart and plant your feet firmly on the ground with toes pointed straight ahead.

Keep your shoulders stacked over your hips, your chin parallel to the floor and your ears aligned with your shoulders. Now that should feel better… if you have to sit.

Whenever you can, walk and talk; just make it a big YES and do it.

When we walk and talk shoulder to shoulder and eliminate the barrier of a desk or table, the conversations become more real, more authentic. And when we move (walk), endorphins flow through our systems and creativity increases. What is distracting you and what is your bigger, more important YES?

It's time to intentionally use your YES to leverage more focus. Say NO to frivolous distractions and become a Get-It-Done POI.

"It's not just about making great products, but great products that enrich people's lives."

—Tim Cook

Week 8
Enrich Lives

Think of your work as more than a job, a paycheck, an impressive corporate title, or a cool corner office. Think beyond the stuff.

The late, Steve Jobs is famous for saying, "People want happier and better lives. Don't just push products. Enrich lives." And even more recently with the introduction of the iPhone 6 and the Apple Watch, Tim Cook continued Job's legacy with this question:

"What are you doing to enrich lives?"

What's the cause, the calling and the significance of your work, your leadership, your parenting, and your impact in this life? Again, what are you doing to enrich lives?

Why is this important to anyone wanting to reimagine their brand? It's important because we are multidimensional people and one life dimension that brings meaning and fulfillment is purpose. As a people we are drawn to, motivated and driven by purpose—a cause, a calling that is more than a job, an important sounding corporate title, or even a hotshot car in the garage.

We're not saying it's bad to have or want these things. We're saying these things, in and of themselves, can be unfulfilling. These things devoid of purpose will lead to empty success.

For almost 30 years we've been committed to writing about companies that are known as the BEST places where the BEST people can do their BEST work to make the world (or at least their corner of the world) BETTER.

Why?

Because deeply planted in all of us is a desire to make the world better, to leave a legacy, to add value, and to make a difference by enriching and improving the lives of others. We all want to leave our own mark in one way or another.

Life isn't just about big houses, cool cars and designer brands, and business isn't just about market share, ROI and the bottom line.

People in general, employees, our kids, and specifically, millennials—the $200 billion economy—we are all far more excited to buy and work for a cause that makes the world better.

Most of us will spend more money and give more time for products and services that enrich us, ones that create happier and better lives for ourselves and our families.

Without a heart,
it's just a machine.

Who can deny that it's cool to enrich and improve the world? Who can deny that it's cool to do epic stuff?

BEST place companies prove over and over again that people want to work for a company that is making the world better. Southwest Airlines (SWA) blazed the trail for creating a cause-driven corporate culture before it was cool to be cause-focused.

Southwest Airlines democratized the skies by defining the company as more than an airline. Southwest defined its people as "freedom fighters" — who make it possible through low fares for ordinary people to GO places, SEE things and DO things they never dreamed possible before SWA lowered fares across the country.

Being in the Business of Freedom has inspired epic acts of service and epic acts of innovation within SWA. Making flying affordable to all people is the cause that drives people in all positions to look for ways to improve service and lower costs without compromising safety, service, security or schedule.

Thinking and acting like a freedom fighter inspired a new flight attendant to question the cost of putting logos on trash bags:

"Do we really need to print logos on our trash bags? We are just throwing them away, and all the passengers on our flights know they are on SWA."

Her question saved Southwest $350,000 a year, and it is just one example of how a cost savings in one area allows SWA to keep costs low and offer continued GO, SEE, DO Freedom to all passengers and employees.

Blake Mycoskie, Chief Shoe Giver and Founder of TOMS shoes started the business based upon the power of cause. TOMS One for One movement—buy a pair of shoes (and now an even more extensive line of products, ranging from sunglasses, to candles and more) and a child in a third world country gets a pair too. Through the TOMS One for One movement with every product we purchase TOMS will help a person in need.

When you can define a business as a cause more than just pushing/selling products or services and if it's about enriching lives people will opt in because they WANT to not because they have to.

People will give more time energy and creative capital to a cause that is enriching lives.

And the **Healthy Home Company** gets it too. Imagine the benefit of using personal and home cleaning products that are toxic-free—harmless to our homes, harmless to our environment, and harmless to us when we use them. Imagine using products that clean as well as, if not better than, the chemically laced products currently available in retail stores today… those currently under your sink and in your home.

Most of us don't even realize that the products we use every day to clean ourselves, our homes and our children are laced with 80,000 chemicals known to cause birth defects, diseases and disorders.

Here's another startling fact: It only takes 26 seconds for a chemical to go from our skin directly into our bloodstream. Living toxic-free should and can be priceless. It doesn't have to be complicated, overly expensive and totally disruptive to your life today. The Healthy Home Company (HHC) is a cause,  and the cause (living toxic-free) is inspiring a movement of like-minded people who are enriching lives one home at a time. The people of HHC are making a toxic-free lifestyle simple, fun, cost effective and, ultimately, priceless to you, your family, your home and your community.

Cause inspires passion. Do you have a passion for selling—the company, its products and services, and yourself? In business and in life, EVERYONE must sell.

Whether you are the ambassador of first impressions who answers the phones or the CEO, do people believe that you believe in what you are doing and in what you are selling?

When you can define a business as a cause, more than just pushing/selling products or services, and if it's about enriching lives, people will opt in because they WANT to not because they have to. People will give more time, energy and creative capital to a cause that is enriching lives.

A cause inspires you to want to step into the breach. When the going gets tough (and it will), are you known for jumping in the boat and grabbing an oar vs. doing a subtle disappearing act. Whether it's going over a pitch; going the extra mile for a frustrated customer, a sick child, or a needy neighbor; or running for pizza because your team is working late, stepping into the breach is about seeing the gap and filling it. It is about maniacal focus vs. feeble commitments! It's about enriching lives one person at a time.

Karen Shadders, an Executive at Wegmans, one of the BEST Companies to work for in America, says, "Every day it is my goal to keep our three company values top of mind and to live them boldly. They are my big YES."

We asked her, how do you do it? Every day she takes the same route to work and on that route she has identified a visual trigger point that reminds her to reflect on the values and walk into the office conscious of how to live them boldly.

Can you come up with a visual trigger point or a daily ritual that will remind you to live your values, to help others see the value in the work they do, and to talk about how you collectively enrich lives?

What will that trigger point or ritual be for you?

ASKHOLE

...a person who constantly asks for your advice, yet never really listens to it or applies it.

Week 9
Be Interested... And Interesting!

Interested = caring, asking questions, probing to learn, understand and add value.

Interested people create space for others to talk. Do you invite and offer space for others to have a voice?

Interesting = having a unique point of view, strong convictions, a clear voice.

Are you someone worth talking to? Talking about? Would you want to spend an evening over dinner with you? Have you acquired a body of knowledge that you can apply to many things going on in the world?

How would you rate yourself on a scale of 1-7 in terms of being interested and interesting? (1 = low/7 = high).

What do you want to work on? Being more interested or more interesting.

How do you become more interested?

Peter Drucker is famous for saying, "The leader of the past knows how to TELL and the leader of today knows how to ASK."

Have you built a brand, a promise of a pending experience, where people know you will ask and listen to understand? More pointed … do you listen with sincere interest?

Most people do NOT listen to understand, they listen to reply.
Are you guilty?

A great example of how to ask and how to listen for understanding is what Jackie experienced while doing an event in Jamaica for LensCrafters. The company hosted their Diamond Store Managers, the 100 top performers in the company, to celebrate their hard work and to inspire a worldwide culture of continued learning and cross-functional transparency.

The most impressive sessions were hosted by LensCrafters/Luxottica Zone Vice Presidents. All the ZVPs held court on stage and invited the 100 best managers in the company to ASK questions all afternoon in a very open and relaxed format.

Why? In the spirit of building a culture of transparency, collaboration and humility, the ZVPs were demonstrating how difficult it is to know everything that is happening in a global company. This session demonstrated the power of asking as a key to gaining information and growing your network.

MOST PEOPLE
DO NOT LISTEN
WITH THE INTENT
TO UNDERSTAND;
THEY LISTEN
WITH THE INTENT
TO REPLY.

The premise—create a culture of transparency. In a global company, you cannot possibly know it all, so dare to ask (be interested), listen to understand and connect with people (for a refresher on this, go back to the value of a powerful network in Keep Good Company, Strategy #3). Creating a culture where people have the freedom to ask is priceless.

How do you become more interesting?

Interesting people tell interesting stories. People of influence know how to tell stories. Why?

Stories are, and always have been, a powerful teaching tool. This fact has been demonstrated for over 2,000 years. Research shows that stories can increase recall by up to 300 percent! What happens if you place critical data or an important point in an interesting story? If people remember the story, they will most likely remember the point and the data.

Stories are entertaining, they can be replicated and passed on, and they create a common experience. This is why stories can strengthen the unity of a culture. When was the last time you sat around with co-workers and talked about the all-nighter that got the shipment there on time, the heroic customer service comeback or the marketing campaign that blew the doors off the competition? Next time you have something important to share, avoid the temptation to simply quote a fact or put an idea in an email. Put it in a story and be braggadocios. Southwest Airlines, one of the best corporate storytellers in the world, is famous for saying, "It ain't bragging if you've done it!" Brag! Tell your story with passion and confidence.

Practice to become more interesting, practice telling a great story. What important point can you plant in a story to bring it to life and to inspire more recall?

To improve your impact strive for becoming a "7" in interested and a "7" in interesting. Your goal is to strive for a balance of both, to be interesting AND interested.

Listen to understand, not just to reply or tell your own story.

Gifted leaders are BOTH. It is a balancing act and it is worthy of practice.

At the next social or business function you attend, make a conscious choice to:

- Ask first
- Listen to understand
- Strive to build on what you hear
- When you tell, make your points easier to remember by planting them in an interesting story

Week 10
Exercise Daily

It's true… It is easier to stay in shape than it is to get in shape… But don't let NOT being in shape hold you back. Start with a new habit that is doable for you and gradually add to it.

Let us remind ourselves of an earlier point … Sometimes, you have to "Just do it," and move!

Research proves time and time again, that exercise is associated with living longer. Exercise doesn't have to be a rigorous or a long exaggerated workout.

On average, 15 minutes of exercise — anything from walking, running, swimming and even gardening—can lower your mortality. Thirty minutes is better and better yet eventually try to build up to 45 minutes a day. And it doesn't have to be all at once. You can do 15 minutes in the morning, 15 in the afternoon and 15 at night.

And for anyone who dreads the thought of any kind of exercise, perhaps this TED Talk by Emily Balcetis will help. In her talk, she notes that perception is subjective and explains that through research she discovered that some people actually see exercise as more difficult than other people. She offers a simple, free strategy for making exercise look and feel easier. She calls it, "keep your eye on the prize."

So why is exercise so important?

Sitting has become the new smoking for this generation and sitting is also very hazardous to our health. Research shows that on average we sit for 9.3 hours a day which is longer than most people sleep. Sleeping is good for us, but sitting is not.

Too much sitting leads to increases in cancer, heart disease, diabetes and obesity, all of which we can avoid if we get off our bottoms and move.

Look, we're not asking you to engage in a sweat fest if that isn't your style. We're trying to encourage you to just move. If you don't like running … don't do it. We're just suggesting you try until you do find something you like and then do it every day. Research proves that even small, simple changes make a difference in overall well-being.

Bypass the elevator and take the stairs instead. If you make the stairs a habit and use them exclusively, that simple change can help decrease body fat, waist circumference, and cholesterol levels and can increase lung capacity.

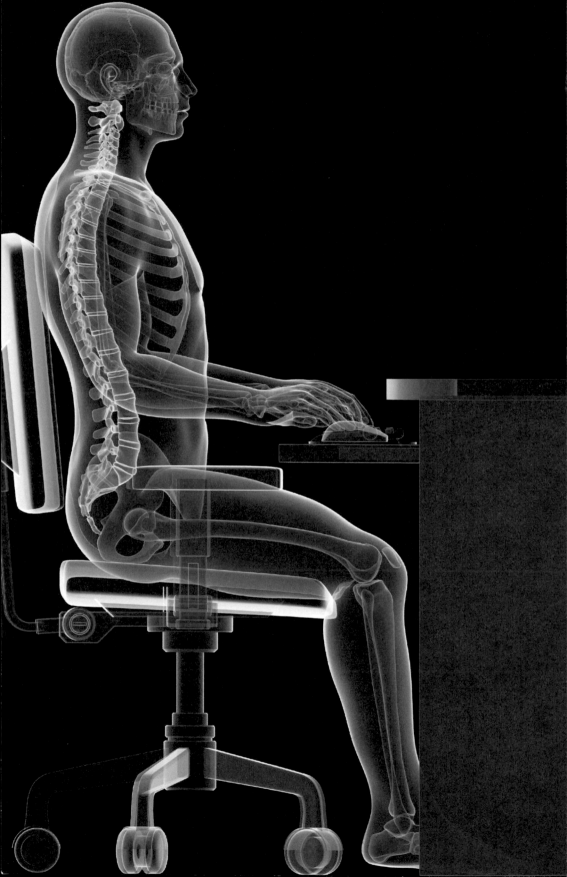

Exercise daily is about finding something you do like. Why not commit to trying a variety of workouts for a month? Try cross fit, yoga, spinning, cycling, swimming, dancing, basketball, or hiking. Try new things until you find a comfortable and fun fit for you.

Even walking is a great choice. Take walking breaks and do walking meetings (for a refresher revisit Say NO!, Strategy #7).

You can burn 60 more calories an hour by standing vs. sitting. If you have a desk job, try a standing workstation. You don't have to transition to a standing station all at once, break up your day and gradually build in more standing time.

Invest in a Fitbit, a Jawbone UP, an Apple Watch, or any form of technology that tracks your steps. Fitness technology will motivate you to move more. It can also be programmed to cue you to get up and move when you are idle or sitting for too long. The technology inspires accountability and encourages us to lean into a lifestyle of living and moving mindfully, purposefully and intentionally.

Or keep it simple. You don't need technology to inspire you to move. Create a workout log. It's a written pat on the back and a workout high five. Record the kind of workout, duration, distance, location, how you felt during and after, plus anything else that helps in encouraging you to keep on moving.

Another idea is to go cold. Gradually build up your temperature tolerance by showering in cold water for a few minutes and then gradually adding more time. It's even easier if you build up a sweat first, Chilly water is a nice way to regulate body temperature post workout to prevent muscle soreness and fatigue. And taking a cold shower can improve circulation, boost your immune system and increase your metabolism. Cold showers can even improve your attitude by stimulating parts of the brain associated with mood.

When you live and move mindfully it is also important to eat mindfully as well. Our bodies are a temple, do you treat yours as such?

Don't diet. Eat mindfully and intentionally. Eat to fuel your body not to soothe your soul. We invite you to learn a bit more on this from neuroscientist Sandra Aamodt. In her 12-minute TED Talk she uses her personal story to frame an important lesson about how our brains manage our bodies as she explores the science behind why dieting not only doesn't work, but is likely to do more harm than good. She suggests ideas for how to live a less diet-obsessed life.

The overall goal here is to sit less, to move more and to be mindful of why we eat, what we eat, how we eat, and even when and where we eat.

When you feel stronger physically through what you do and what you eat, you will have more energy to focus on what it's going to take to be a stand out POI … YOU at your best!

- What do you want to do to move more? What will you do and how often?

- How will you hold yourself accountable? Will you invest in some form of technology or will you create an exercise log?

- What do you need to do to eat more mindfully?

- What do you need to avoid or do differently when it comes to fueling your body?

- When will you start and how will you hold yourself accountable for being more mindful about food choices?

DON'T BE SORRY, CHANGE.

Practice the Art of the Apology

Building a great brand is also about owning mistakes, being willing to admit it when you are wrong, learning how not to repeat your mistake, letting go and moving on.

Our dear friend and the Chief Spiritual Officer of our business is Dr. Ken Blue. He is one of the most grounded in GRACE people we know and thankfully Ken has given us grace-based counsel for our entire lives together.

One important grace-oriented Ken-ism:

"Being right is highly overrated." This has been a great gift to our marriage and family. Not that we have it wired, but we do our best to keep it top of mind in the midst of a heated debate (aka full on fight).

Kevin and I both have graduate degrees in Communications so when we argue it can easily turn into a highly competitive "I'm right, you're wrong debate." We're both trained to use our communications skills and we do. But, if we're not careful those skills can take us out relationally. Sadly, we've lost too many weekends in the pursuit of being right. Ken has encouraged us to practice the art of the apology.

Own the disagreement, say you're sorry, and acknowledge that it's OK to agree to disagree. Then let go of being right and move on.

CAUTION 1:

If you find yourself apologizing for the same thing more than a couple times, it's time to SHOW you're sorry and change. Here is another personal example.

When our kids were young we had a neighborhood carpool. When Jackie traveled Kevin would drive in her place. Well, Kevin, self-admittedly, is notoriously late. And that didn't go over well with a couple of the kids in the carpool.

First day: Kevin shows up late, says, "Sorry!" and off they go. Second day: Kevin shows up late and says, "So sorry!" The neighbor looks at Kevin and says, "Don't be sorry, change!" Our neighbor was right.

Remember, to communicate well (Strategy #3):
"Say what you mean, mean what you say and don't say it mean."

Our neighbor was practicing simple, direct non-emotional communication. The phrase "Don't be sorry, change!" made such an impression on Kevin that we have adopted it as a family motto and practice it regularly in our home.

Feedback.
Reflection.
Insight.

You can let it buckle you...
or you can learn from it,
change and GROW.

Here is a very memorable corporate example. We posted this on our site a while back and still think it is worth sharing here. In July of 2009, Amazon remotely deleted (unauthorized) copies of the books "1984" and "Animal Farm" from users' Kindles. Of course, the move had a "Big Brother-like" feel and left many people angry. We don't think we've ever seen a better example of an apology than this. Way to go Jeff!

> *This is an apology for the way we previously handled illegally sold copies of 1984 and other novels on Kindle. Our "solution" to the problem was stupid, thoughtless, and painfully out of line with our principles. It is wholly self-inflicted, and we deserve the criticism we've received. We will use the scar tissue from this painful mistake to help make better decisions going forward, ones that match our mission.*
>
> *With deep apology to our customers,*
>
> **Jeff Bezos, Founder & CEO, Amazon.com**

Unfortunately, we see so little of this among business leaders and politicians today. Perhaps it's fear that this kind of vulnerability will lead to litigation or worse—a tarnished image. In any case, we suspect that there is a lesson in this for all of us, and we know many were endeared to Amazon because of Jeff's humility and courage to practice the art of the apology.

CAUTION 2:

To be sorry is simply the kick-start of an apology. Changing your behavior to avoid the same mistake again is what matters most. It demonstrates your remorse and paves the way for growing trust again.

And here is a more personal business example. Not too long ago we both spoke for the leaders of a number of luxury resorts and hotels. The CEO did a remarkably vulnerable and gutsy thing, standing alone on a dark stage, under a spot light, in front of 500 direct reports, he pulled a note card out of his pocket and read this list:

- Never satisfied
- Jerk
- Cold
- Aloof
- Thinks he's always right
- Talks too much

- Machiavellian
- Impatient
- Jackass
- Heartless
- Distant
- Calculated

And then looked up and said, "these are names that have been attributed to me in the last couple years. When I took this job, I grossly underestimated the amount of feedback I would receive. I had no idea how much I would get and from so many sources. You can let it buckle you or you can learn to change. You can not lead well with out self-awareness and sometimes self-awareness hurts."

WHAT IF WE RAISED A
NEW GENERATION OF LEADERS WHO COULD
ADMIT WHEN THEY WERE WRONG?

He concluded with a formal apology to the team and committed to work on changing.

We share this because it is a remarkable example of the power of vulnerability, the desire to become self-aware and the art of the apology.

How do you get others to do their best work? Apologize, own your humanness, commit to change and improve your impact.

Once again, this is about WHO you are, about what other people think about you. That's where development and leadership starts. When you lead a team, a family or a company it's critical for you to know WHO you are and be fully aware of the impact AND influence you have on others.

And it's not just about what you're NOT good at, you have to know your strength story too. Do you dare ask:

- What do you like about working with me?

- What don't you like and what would you change?

- Or what if you ask: "What are my most admired qualities and where am I not leveraging them. And what are my fatal flaws?"

When you get feedback don't let it buckle you, reflect, apologize, share and change.

What if we taught our kids The Art of the Apology and raised a new generation of leaders who could admit when they are wrong and commit to improving their impact?

The art of the apology involves owning our mistake; saying we're sorry; changing our behavior; letting go of the screw up, anger and hurt; and most importantly, moving on (shake it off). #poi #personofimpact

Being a stand out POI will require you to CHANGE some ineffective habits.

- Is the need to be right disrupting relationships and tarnishing your brand?

- How and what will you do to change?

- With whom and for what is it in your best interest to let go of the need to be right?

Week 12
Forgive with Grace

"Living the Dream" has become the new saying, the cool new greeting. Is the power of suggestion at play here? Perhaps if I say it enough, you'll believe it, and maybe I'll begin to believe it too.

Living the Dream! WOW, who doesn't want that? We all do, but if we're honest, none of us is always living the dream 24/7. A phrase like that connotes the perfect life—all is great, no problems, no complaints.

Well, none of us lives a perfect life and if you think someone does, here's some breaking news—it's a facade.

If we're honest, we are all self-centered, self-indulgent and self-protective and we're all wounded. Our selfishness and our wounds become baggage that we all bring into our relationships.

When my baggage crashes into your baggage or when my sharp edge grinds against your sharp edge, we hurt each other, and we will. And when we hurt each other we need reconciliation.

Whether we're dealing with conflict in a marriage, family, company, community or nation, we all must have the courage to forgive and seek forgiveness in order to achieve reconciliation.

When someone extends forgiveness, by definition, all resentment, indignation, hurt or anger as a result of a perceived offense, disagreement or mistake, ends.

When someone extends grace, by definition, we become the recipient of something that is generous, free, totally unexpected and feels undeserved.

Forgiveness is a gift, that's why we use the word "grace."

Grace is a free gift. It isn't earned, it is not conditional, it is not dependent upon anything, it's not obligatory—it's free. It is an act of kindness, it is a blessing…neither of which need to be earned.

Ask this…"Is holding onto the anger and hurt hindering my joy and paralyzing me from living my life to the fullest and being able to be the best brand I desire?" If so, your ability to forgive with grace has the potential to be personally cleansing and professionally refreshing.

- What are you holding onto that is becoming toxic to you and your brand?

- Who do you need to forgive with grace? How and when will you share your forgiveness?

"For our nation to heal and become a more humane place, we had to embrace our enemies as well as our friends. True enduring peace—between countries, within a country, within a community, within a family—requires real reconciliation between former enemies and even between loved ones who have struggled with one another.

If peace is our goal, there can be no future without forgiveness."

— Desmond Tutu

Being able to let go, forgive (without expectation) and move on frees you of leaky behavior and paves the way to being a stand out POI, free from toxic spills. Now let's unpack how.

Forgiveness is a choice

When Nelson Mandela became South Africa's first democratically-elected President, he established the Truth and Reconciliation Commission. The purpose of the commission was to move South Africa beyond the cycles of retribution and violence that had plagued so many other countries during their transitions from oppression to democracy.

The commission granted perpetrators of political crimes the opportunity to appeal for amnesty by giving a full and truthful account of their actions and, if they so chose, the opportunity to ask for forgiveness.

The commission also gave victims of political crimes a chance to tell their stories, hear confessions, and thus unburden themselves from the pain and suffering they had experienced.

Forgiveness might sound like another one of those touch-feely concepts you read about in self-help books. To you it may seem weak, like you're being a wimp and letting people off the hook.

"Forgiveness is unlocking the door to set someone free and realizing you were the prisoner!"
—*Max Lucado*

Forgiveness is not about slipping into denial or playing "pretend."

It's not about acting like everything is OK when it isn't. There are no quick fixes. The deeper the pain, the longer the healing takes. That is why there is so much patience, perseverance and hard work involved in forgiveness.

Forgiveness requires humility, strength and vulnerability.

Forgiveness is one of the gutsiest things you'll ever do! Gandhi once said, "Forgiveness is the attribute of the strong." Do not let anger take root and wreak havoc in your life.

We cannot control the actions, behaviors and feelings of others, so holding out for others to change first may not be in your best interest. It's gutsy, awkward and vulnerable, but sometimes we have to do the changing. And hopefully through our example, our choices and changing our responses to the offenses of others we can effect more reconciliation in our lives.

Our lives will change when we put forgiveness and grace together.

When we generously, freely, unexpectedly and even undeservingly release all our resentment, indignation, anger and hurt from an offense, disagreement or mistake, we are released and the recipient of our forgiveness is free and absolved as well.

Is it easy? No way! It is the toughest brand building strategy of the twelve.

Why is it so important? Because you cannot be your best and reimagine your brand when you are harboring the hurt from old wounds, bitterness, or unresolved offenses.

Why is forgiveness so hard?

People will let you down. Life isn't fair!

…your SPOUSE won't measure up to your expectations;

…your KIDS will disrespect you by breaking the rules;

…your FRIENDS will betray you;

…your BOSS will act like a jerk and hurt you.

Unfortunately, if you feed and nourish this disappointment long enough, it will deeply root and grow. There is no payoff for carrying anger and resentment around for even a short period. It's emotionally draining, it distracts you from adding value to the people you love, and it derails you from doing the things that make you an effective, go-to, get-it-done person.

Over the long haul, anytime you allow someone else's dysfunction to weigh on you and to shape your attitude, you disempower yourself, not them. You actually empower their dysfunction by allowing it to impact and reshape you.

4 Awakening questions:

1. Would you purposely drink strychnine or breathe carbon monoxide?

2. Would you put 30 pounds of rock in a backpack before hiking 10 miles out of the Grand Canyon?

3. Would you leave an infected wound to heal by itself?

4. Would you invite someone who's hurt you many times to coffee for another round of abuse?

These questions are ludicrous, but isn't that what we do when we harbor hostility and carry resentment around for a long time? Trying to forget about the hurt someone has inflicted upon you without actually forgiving them is like expecting the wound to heal on its own—it won't. We deepen the wound, exaggerate the pain and invite in more hurt!

WHAT SPILLS OUT WHEN SOMEONE BUMPS INTO YOU?

Fail to forgive and the ANGER will eat you up inside.

Refusing to forgive is like strapping on a huge backpack filled with past hurts. Every time someone makes a mistake, fails to meet an expectation or offends you, you throw it into the backpack. The problem of course is that the backpack gets heavier and heavier, and carrying it out of the canyon becomes virtually impossible. Yet, we all know people who are weighted down by carrying this toxic waste around for weeks, months and years—even to their graves.

Resentment is like venom that gets into your bloodstream. If it stays there long enough, it will eventually eat away at your heart.

Forgiveness is first for you. It's about releasing you from something that will eat you alive and will destroy your joy and your ability to live, love and lead fully, freely and more openly.

Not "letting go" of anger and ruminating over past hurts is no different than inviting someone to hurt you over and over again.

Holding on to anger, resentment or bitterness is more harmful to you than the one you hold the anger toward. Anger, bitterness and resentment are toxic; they are very much like a cancer that wreaks havoc within your body.

> *"Holding onto anger is like drinking poisn and expecting the other persion to die"*
> — *Buddha*

Although your anger may not kill you literally, harbored anger will leak when you least expect it. Leaky behavior is hazardous to your brand, your reputation and your relationships!

Why do we call it leaky behavior? Think about it, if someone bumps into you when you are holding a cup of coffee, your coffee is likely to spill. We are like the cup, if we are holding anger and someone bumps into us, anger will leak.

What is likely to spill out of you when someone bumps into you?

Be careful! Holding onto anger is like picking up a hot coal with the intention of throwing it at someone, but in doing so you get hurt. Holding onto anger weakens our spirits, tires our souls, and clouds our perspectives.

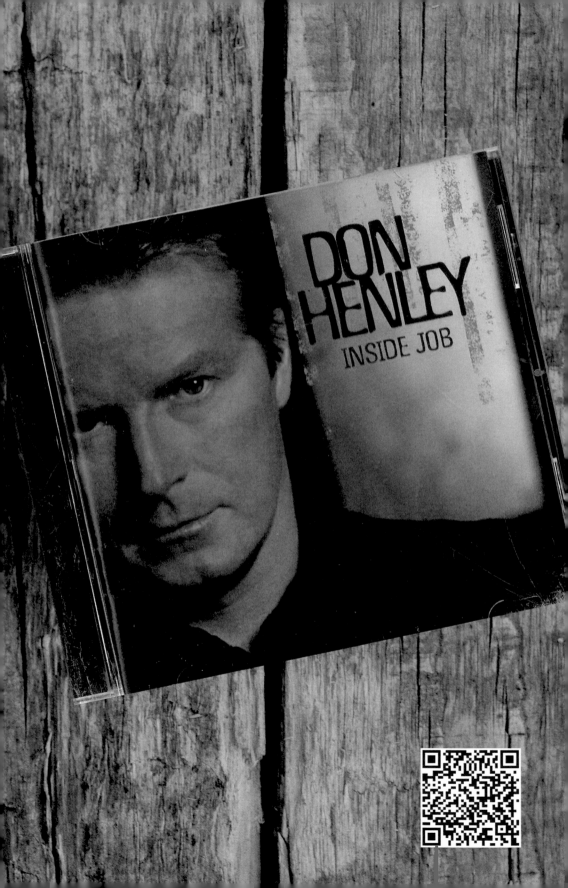

Forgiveness is the ♥ of the matter!

We are huge fans of the Eagles and Don Henley. Henley is a famous American singer-songwriter, producer, drummer and one of the founding band member and lead vocalists for the Eagles. Henley is well known for singing the lead vocals on Eagles hits, "Witchy Woman, Desparado, Best of My Love, One of These Nights, Hotel California, Life in the Fast Lane, and The Long Run." During the Eagles break up between 1980-1994, Henley pursued a solo career and it was then that he produced "The Heart of the Matter."

Join us in better understanding the power of forgiveness as we unpack the lyrics of Don Henley's song "The Heart of the Matter."

And I thought of all the bad luck and the struggles we went through and how I lost me and you lost you.

Life will confront you with ample opportunities to forgive, and when we fail to respond something inside of us dies a little bit. We become hardened, more calloused and we lose a part of ourselves.

What are those voices outside love's open door, make us throw off our contentment and beg for something more?

Life will tempt you to look beyond the contentment of an incredible relationship and beg for something more. But it rarely delivers.

The more I know, the less I understand, all the things I thought I knew, I'm learning again.

Whether it's an intimate relationship, a friendship or working relationship, it's easy to assume that we know what it means to love, what love looks like—until that love is tested. Then, the more we know the less we understand. And, we learn all over again that deep relationships can't exist without forgiveness.

I've been tryin' to get down to the heart of the matter.

The truth of the matter is that the things of the heart—like forgiveness—aren't always logical. They don't always fit into a nice, neat formula. To forgive and be forgiven often comes from deep emotional places. Is it any wonder that when we try to understand it through the eyes of logic our thoughts scatter?

But my will gets weak and my thoughts seem to scatter.

But our WILL gets weak. Forgiveness is hard! That's why we have to draw upon a strength greater than our own.

When we step into that vulnerable spot of knowing how much we've been forgiven, something in us begins to stir, to move toward forgiving.

I think it's about forgiveness, forgiveness even if, even if you don't love
me anymore.

Forgiveness is not conditional upon you loving me. It's not a feeling. It's often a gutsy, visceral decision of the will.

And even if forgiveness won't always bring a relationship back, it is one of the keys to understanding what went wrong and then having the freedom to move on.

… People filled with rage we all need a little tenderness how can love survive in such a
graceless age?

We live in an uncivil world—a world where we do so much harm to one another. We've got blame and judgment down, but what people long for is a little empathy, a bit of tenderness—forgiveness.

The trust and self-assurance that lead to happiness

They're the very things we kill, pride and competition cannot fill these empty arms
And the work I put between us doesn't keep me warm

You can trade trust, self-assurance and vulnerability for pride, competition and control, but they won't fill the emptiness. Trust and grace, not pride, are the keys to happiness.

There are people in your life who've come and gone, they let you down, you know
they've hurt your pride.

Life isn't fair. There are people who have come and gone and who will come again—who let you down. You can't avoid that and you can't always control it.

Oh, you can mitigate it by building walls of self-defense and self-protection—but then you miss out on life.

You better put it behind you; 'cause life goes on.

You keep carryin' that anger, it'll eat you up inside baby,

Let the ANGER linger and it will eat you up inside, so you gotta deal with it and then put it behind you—or it will consume you, break you and weaken you.

Not long after hearing Henley sing this song, India Arie, another very gifted singer-song-writer and Grammy winner performed her own very powerful rendition of the Heart of the Matter. After hearing Arie's, Henley said he liked her version better. You decide, here is Arie's performance for the North Sea Jazz Festival.

It's the HEART of the matter ... Fail to get this right and we will never have what we need and desire—deep, meaningful relationships—and we will have great difficulty leading, being a stand out POI.

Whoever THEY are for you, we challenge you not to let THEM lock you behind the walls of anger and resentment.

Here's what we want you to do:

Conduct an audit of your gifts and talents, who are you? Think about the potential you have to make a mark in the world.

Ask: *Is the bitterness you have toward THEM worth compromising all this potential?*

Look at the loved ones in your life who mean something to you. Is your propensity to harbor anger worth the toxic spillover and negative energy that infects their lives?

Don't let another day go by; seize the moment. Write the letter, schedule the meeting, make the call, and take a step toward freedom by getting it "right" with those who have hurt you and those you have hurt as well.

Most of us are afraid to die because we have not fully lived; perhaps we should push fear and anger aside and live more fully, more freely and more joyfully.

Over the years we've heard some powerful messages around being your best. We've paraphrased a number of them in our book BOOM! and this one is worth sharing:

As we get older, we learn that life just isn't fair. You will risk and fail. People you count on will overpromise and under

deliver and the one individual you thought you could trust more than anyone in this world will probably let you down. You will invest time, talent and money in those who will either squander the investment or show no gratitude. Your heart will eventually be broken and the pain will seem unbearable. You will also hurt others and disappoint those you love—remember how it feels. At some point you will wake up horrified and wonder, "What have I done with my life?" because time waits for no one!

So don't take yourself too seriously. Love like you've never been hurt. Learn like you will live forever and live like you will die tomorrow. Every sixty seconds you spend agitated and upset is a moment of peace, joy and "aliveness" you'll never get back.

Now What?

Beware! People will doubt you and cause you to doubt yourself. People will ignore you, laugh at you, or fight you. BUT, if you hold true to a reimagined you, you will win!

What is holding you back?   Who is dragging you down?

Stay focused. Say NO to anyone and anything that is dragging you down and holding you back.

The script is blank, the options are many, the focus is clear. YOU are the CEO of your future. It's time to get started. Be strategic and be a standout POI!

12 POI Strategies

- [ ] Self-Evaluate
- [ ] List Goals
- [ ] Keep Good Company
- [ ] Become a Connoisseur
- [ ] Communicate Well
- [ ] Manage Your Mind
- [ ] Say NO! Get-It-Done
- [ ] Enrich Lives
- [ ] Be Interested...And Interesting!
- [ ] Exercise Daily
- [ ] Practice the Art of the Apology
- [ ] Forgive with Grace

Jackie and Kevin Freiberg

Are bestselling authors and founders of the San Diego Consulting Group Inc. The Freibergs are dedicated to helping leaders create Best Places where the Best People can do their Best Work to make the world Better. Both have Ph.D.'s and teach part-time at the University of San Diego, School of Leadership and Education Sciences.

In their international bestseller ***NUTS! Southwest Airlines Crazy Recipe for Business and Personal Success***, Kevin and Jackie uncovered the strategies that created the greatest success story in the history of commercial aviation. NUTS! was followed by:

GUTS! Companies that Blow the Doors Off Business-as-usual;

BOOM! 7 Choices for Blowing the Doors Off Business-as-usual;

NANOVATION: How a Little Car Can Teach the World to Think Big, the inside story of one of the greatest innovations in the auto industry since the Model-T. It's also a roadmap for expanding your capacity to innovate and making innovation part of your cultural DNA; and

DO SOMETHING NOW, three simple words that will change your organization—change your life. The scarcest resource in organizations right now is not money, talent, ideas or power; it's people who DO, people who add value and get things done. DSN inspires Dreamers to become Doers. Everyone wants to add value and this book shows you how.

The Freibergs speak on **leadership**, **innovation** and **change** all over the world. They have a global practice including firms in Europe, Japan, South Africa, India, Central and South America, as well as companies throughout the United States and Canada.

We want to hear from you at kevinandjackie@freibergs.com

jackiefreiberg

kevinfreiberg

Made in the USA
Middletown, DE
18 October 2017